Amazing Animals
WOLVES

Jen Green

W
FRANKLIN WATTS
LONDON•SYDNEY

An Appleseed Editions book

First published in 2010 by Franklin Watts

Franklin Watts
338 Euston Road, London NW1 3BH

Franklin Watts Australia
Level 17/207 Kent St, Sydney, NSW 2000

© 2010 Appleseed Editions

Appleseed Editions Ltd
Well House, Friars Hill, Guestling, East Sussex TN35 4ET

Created by Q2AMedia
Editor: Katie Dicker
Art Director: Harleen Mehta
Designer: Dibakar Acharjee and Shilpi Sarkar
Picture Researcher: Maria Janet
Line Artist: Rama Krishna
Colouring Artist: Abhijeet Sharma

ISBN 978 1 4451 0007 4

Dewey classification: 599.7'73

All words in **bold** can be found in the Glossary on pages 30–31.

Website information is correct at the time of going to press. However, the publishers cannot
accept liability for any information or links found on third-party websites.

A CIP catalogue for this book is available from the British Library.

Picture credits
t=top b=bottom c=centre l=left r=right
Cover images: Zorro/Dreamstime, Dreamstime

Denis Pepin/Istockphoto: Title page, Amanda Rohde/Istockphoto: Contents page, Motor-Presse Syndication/Photolibrary: 4,
Tanya Kozlovsky/Shutterstock: 5, Ronald Wittek/Photolibrary: 6, Thomas Kitchin & Victoria Hurst/Photolibrary: 7,
David W Hamilton/Photolibrary: 8, Takiev Alexander/Shutterstock: 9t, James Urbach/Photolibrary: 9b, K Wothe/
Photolibrary: 10, Mikael Wahlberg/Photolibrary: 11t, Mike Robinson/Photolibrary: 11b, Ronald Wittek/Photolibrary: 12,
Dmitrij/Dreamstime: 13t, Joe McDonald/NHPA: 14, Mark Hamblin/Photolibrary: 15, Steven Kazlowski/Photolibrary: 16,
Michael Sewell/Photolibrary: 17, Eyal Bartov/Photolibrary: 18, T Kitchin & V Hurst/NHPA: 19, Denis Pepin/Istockphoto: 20,
Steven Kazlowski/Photolibrary: 21, Christian Heinrich/Photolibrary: 22, Gisela Delpho/Photolibrary: 23,
The Bridgeman Art Library/Photolibrary: 24, Jeff & Alexa Henry/Photolibrary: 25, Martin Harvey/Photolibrary: 26,
Mary Lee Woodward/Istockphoto: 27, FloridaStock/Shutterstock: 28, Michael DeYoung/Photolibrary: 29,
Takiev Alexander/Shutterstock: 31.

Q2AMedia Art Bank: 13.

Printed in China

Franklin Watts is a division of Hachette Children's Books,
an Hachette Livre UK company.
www.hachettelivre.co.uk

Contents

Fierce hunters

Mean and menacing, with shaggy fur and sharp teeth... that's how many people see wolves. Wolves used to be feared as ferocious, meat-eating hunters. But wolves have a gentler side, too. They are loyal, affectionate and among the world's most intelligent animals.

Sharp canine tooth

The wolf family

Wolves are **predators** – they kill other animals for food. Their main weapons are the long, pointed fangs in the front of their jaws, which they use to seize **prey**. These teeth are called canines, and they give the wolf family its name, the **canids**. Coyotes, jackals and dingoes are closely related to the wolf. Foxes and wild dogs are more distant relatives.

When a wolf snarls, you can see its canine teeth. Wolves, wild dogs and foxes all have long, sharp canines.

4

One species

Wolves are creatures of the north. They were once found right across North America, Europe and Asia, but now they are much rarer. There is only one **species** (or type) of wolf – the grey wolf. But grey wolves that live in different **habitats**, such as forests and deserts, look a little different to one another. Wolves are unusual in that they are able to **breed** with close relatives such as coyotes and domestic dogs. This results in cross-breeds, such as coy-wolves and wolf-dogs.

MAN'S BEST FRIEND?

People see wolves as enemies. But 'man's best friend', the domestic dog, is actually descended from the wolf. Dogs were bred from wolves about 12,000 years ago. Over the centuries, people bred dogs to do different work, such as guarding or hunting. There are now more than 400 different breeds of dog.

The wolf-like husky was bred to pull sledges in the Arctic

 All dogs – from the miniature poodle to the giant St Bernard – are descended from the wolf.

Living together

Wolves are very sociable creatures. Almost all wolves spend their lives in a group called a **pack**. The main purpose of the pack is for hunting. The wolf pack also provides a safe place to rear the young.

Pack hunters

As predators, wolves go after all sorts of prey. Their favourite prey are large, hoofed animals, such as elk, moose and caribou (reindeer). These big beasts will provide a meal for many hunters, but they are powerful, with sharp hooves and horns or antlers. Hunting in a pack allows wolves to target large prey. Single wolves could never tackle these creatures on their own.

 As part of a team, a wolf is able to kill prey up to ten times its own weight.

Pecking order

Most packs contain eight to twelve wolves. The pack is well organised, with a strict **hierarchy** or 'pecking order'. The strongest, most experienced male and female are the leaders. Scientists call these the **'alpha' wolves**. They are the only wolves allowed to breed. The other pack members are usually their children – young **cubs** and wolves of up to three years old. Outsiders are sometimes allowed to join the pack.

The alpha male takes the lead in hunting and defending the group. He decides when and where to go hunting. The alpha female helps to keep the other wolves in line. Large packs may have another pair of wolves who are second in command. These are called **beta wolves**.

LITTLE AND LARGE

The smallest wolf packs contain just two or three animals. The largest pack ever recorded held 36 wolves. This was in Alaska, where wolves go after large prey such as caribou and musk oxen. In general, the biggest wolf packs form in areas that contain the biggest prey animals.

Wolves in a pack have strong bonds. When pack members meet, they whine, lick faces and bury their noses in each other's fur.

Sounds and signals

Good communication is the key to success in the wolf pack. Wolves 'talk' to one another using sounds, scents and body language. Loud, eerie howls send long-distance messages.

Alpha wolves will outstare junior pack members

Body language

Wolves use body language to show their rank within the pack. The alpha male and female stand tall with their ears pricked and heads and tails held high. Younger or weaker dogs show their junior rank by cringing with ears laid back and tails tucked between their legs. If a junior animal challenges a top wolf by snarling, the leader snarls back ferociously. The junior dog may roll on its back or beg for food to show it is backing down.

Alpha wolves stand tall, with their ears pricked, so they look as big as possible.

Long-distance communication

Wolves talk to each other up close using yips, growls, barks and other noises. Howling is used for long-distance communication. When one wolf begins to howl, all the others join in. Each animal has a different voice, so wolves can identify distant pack members. Wolves howl as they gather before hunting. They also howl to warn away rival packs. The eerie howl of a wolf can carry 10 kilometres or more.

Wolves lift their nose in the air to howl.

FACIAL EXPRESSIONS

Scientists have discovered that wolves have at least 20 different **facial** expressions. A wolf pricks its ears and bares its teeth to threaten another. By laying its ears back and 'grinning' with its teeth hidden, a junior wolf says: 'I give in, you are stronger'. Dogs use many of the same expressions and body language.

 This wolf is bearing its teeth to scare another creature away.

Fast and fearless

Wolves are lean, strong and tough – a deadly combination for a hunter. With their long, muscular legs, they are fast movers and almost tireless. Their powerful jaws and sharp canines are used to seize their prey.

Marathon runners

Like all canids, wolves run on their toes. They are not the fastest sprinters, but can keep on the move for hours at a steady pace without tiring. A wolf can manage a top speed of 45 kph for a short distance, to grab fleeing prey. Wolves can also dodge and swerve after prey such as deer and rabbits. With their strong back legs, they can clear 4-metre fences. They are good swimmers, too, and sometimes take to water to capture their prey.

Wolves are speedy and supple, which helps them to overtake their prey.

Strong, slender legs

Bushy tail helps with balance when running

Powerful shoulders

Sleek and deadly

Wolves have very powerful jaws and a long muzzle. As well as long canines, they have scissor-like shearing teeth, called carnassial teeth, at the back of their jaws. These teeth slice through flesh. From its pointed nose to the tip of its long tail, a wolf is sleek and **streamlined**, so it can run fast through tangled undergrowth.

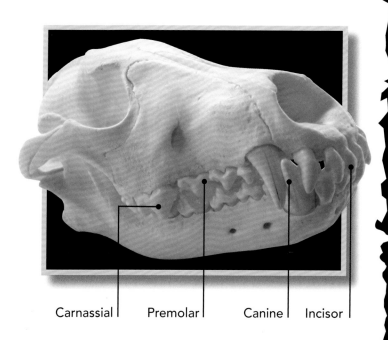

Carnassial | Premolar | Canine | Incisor

Warm fur

The wolf's coat has two types of hairs. Long, coarse hairs called **guard hairs** keep out wind, rain and snow. Soft, dense underfur keeps the wolf snug and warm, even in freezing temperatures.

Wolves have four types of teeth: small incisors, long canines, premolars and molars to cut or crunch bone and scissor-like carnassials.

When wolves run, they place their feet in a straight line to make a narrow trail.

ON THE RUN

A trotting wolf pack can keep up a steady pace of 38 kph for hours. It is not unusual for a pack to cover 200 kilometres in a day. Scientists studying one pack in Alaska found the wolves travelled 805 kilometres in a month – that's about 27 kilometres a day.

Super senses

Wolves are able to hunt day or night thanks to their sharp senses. A wolf's senses are similar to those of a dog. A wolf has a very large brain to interpret all the information gathered by its senses. Dogs are intelligent, but wolves have an even bigger brain.

A world of smells

Wolves mainly track their prey using their sharp sense of smell. The wolf's sensitive nose can identify literally thousands of different smells. Its world is a patchwork of scents that act like landmarks on a journey. The wolf remembers all these smells to build up a 'scent map' in its head.

TRACKING A TRAIL

A wolf can pick up the scent of a deer 2 kilometres away. By sniffing a scent trail it can tell what type of animal has passed, and whether it was sick or injured. It knows how long ago it passed, and whether it was already being stalked by another wolf.

Wolves can follow the scent of its prey for many kilometres, even in the snow.

Eyes and ears

Wolves are good at seeing moving objects, but find it difficult to spot an animal that 'freezes' in its tracks and keeps quite still. Wolves have a wide **field of vision** to see all around. The back of their eyes also reflects light to help them to see in moonlight. If a wolf is caught in a car's headlights, its slanting eyes seem to give off an eerie glow.

Wolves can hear very high sounds we cannot hear. This super sense allows them to hear the rustle of distant deer moving quietly through the forest. If your hearing was that good, you would be able to hear the sound of a ticking watch fifteen paces away.

All the wolf's main senses are on its head.

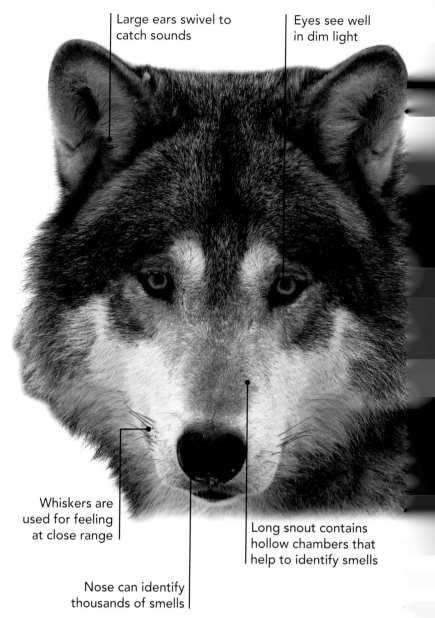

Large ears swivel to catch sounds

Eyes see well in dim light

Whiskers are used for feeling at close range

Nose can identify thousands of smells

Long snout contains hollow chambers that help to identify smells

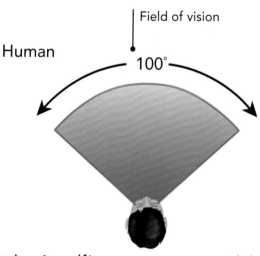

Human

Field of vision

100°

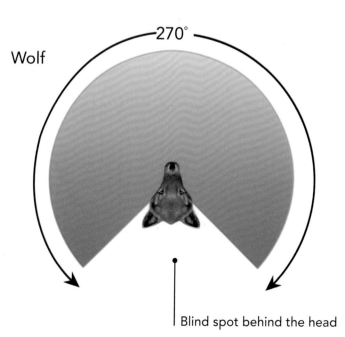

Wolf

270°

Blind spot behind the head

A wolf's eyes are more widely spaced than a person's, and set high on its head. This gives it a very wide field of vision.

A deer hunt

Wolves are carnivores – they eat an all-meat diet if they can. If a wolf gets very hungry it will eat plants and berries. The wolf pack acts as a team to track, stalk, chase and finally bring down a large beast such as an elk or a deer.

A pack of wolves chases the scent of another meal.

Stalking prey

A pack of wolves is hunting at dusk on a snowy landscape. At last they catch the scent of a deer herd **grazing** several kilometres away. The wolves approach their prey cautiously, keeping to the cover of rocks and bushes. They are careful to stay upwind of the herd so the deer don't catch their scent. As they get closer, the wolves single out a young deer as an easy victim.

Closing for the kill

Like a top sports team, the wolves take different roles in the chase that follows. A few swift wolves dart ahead to separate the deer from its herd. Flankers follow the animal as it twists and turns. As it begins to tire, the wolves close in. They snap at the deer's sides and it grows weak from fright and loss of blood. Finally it trips and topples over. A strong wolf such as the alpha male kills it with a bite to the nose or throat.

RARE SUCCESS

Even hunting as a team, nine out of ten wolf hunts end in failure. The wolves will give up the chase if an animal proves too strong or speedy. They won't risk getting injured. Luckily, wolves can go for several days without food, as long as they have water to drink.

Wolves eat every part of their prey – flesh, skin, bones and fur.

Lonely life

Wolves spend most of their lives in the safety of a pack, but some wolves have to survive on their own. This mostly happens when young wolves leave the group to set up a new pack. Or sometimes, an old or sickly wolf is turned out of the pack and left to fend for itself.

Struggle for survival

For a lone wolf, life is one long struggle for survival. Without a pack it cannot hunt large prey. So it goes after smaller creatures, such as hares, mice and birds. It will also eat dead meat and fruit if very hungry. It may approach towns and villages to steal scraps from rubbish dumps.

This lone wolf is feeding on a dead moose it has hidden in the snow.

SAVING IT FOR LATER

If a lone wolf is lucky enough to make a good kill it eats its fill, then hides the rest for later. This is called **caching**. The wolf may stash the meat under rocks or snow.

Keep out!

Wolf packs hunt in a home patch called a **territory** – where there is plenty of prey to eat. A lone wolf is not strong enough to set up a territory. It is forced to hunt in areas not taken by other wolves, where the hunting is poor. Lone wolves have to cover ten or twenty times as much ground as other wolves, to find enough food.

Joining forces

Lone wolves are shy and wary, particularly of other wolves. If a single wolf is caught in a pack's territory, the wolves may tear it to pieces. It will move quickly and quietly across pack land. In a safe, lonely spot a lone wolf may start to howl. If another wolf answers, the pair approach cautiously. They may start a new pack together.

Wolves mark the edges of their territory with urine to warn other wolves away. This is called scent-marking.

A lone wolf is always alert and wary

Desert and forest

Grey wolves are able to live in many different habitats, including forests, deserts, mountains, grasslands and the Arctic **tundra**. Wolves generally live in remote places where there are few people. They are tough and hardy – born survivors.

Suited to surroundings

Wolves that live in different habitats have developed features that help them survive in their particular surroundings. Over many years, slightly different types of wolf have developed. These are called **subspecies**. Scientists have identified up to 30 subspecies of grey wolves, such as Arctic wolves, desert wolves and forest wolves.

Large ears give off heat like mini-radiators to keep the wolf cool

Yellow eyes

Bird caught as prey

Desert wolves hunt alone or in small packs to catch birds and rodents.

Desert wolves

Desert wolves live in dry places and rocky scrublands in Mexico and the Middle East. Their pale, tawny-coloured coat blends in with the sand and rocks. The pale colour also reflects sunlight, which helps them to keep cool. Desert wolves rest in the shade of rocks during the heat of the day and hunt at night when temperatures can be freezing cold.

Timber wolves

Wolves are probably most at home in northern forests. In the USA, forest wolves are called timber wolves. These medium-sized wolves have black, grey, pale or reddish fur – colours that blend in with leaves and bark in the shadowy forest. Timber wolves like to hunt large prey such as moose, elk or white-tailed deer. They also catch smaller creatures – beavers, snowshoe hares and birds.

The timber wolf's fur blends in with the forest. These wolves hunt in medium-size packs of five to ten animals.

The white wolf

The Arctic wolf manages to survive in one of the harshest habitats on Earth – the treeless plains of the north, known as the tundra. This hostile place is covered with snow for much of the year. Winters are long, dark and bitterly cold.

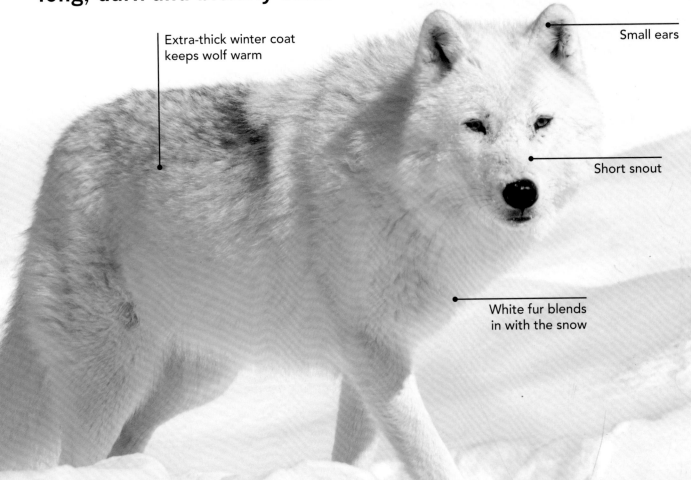

Extra-thick winter coat keeps wolf warm

Small ears

Short snout

White fur blends in with the snow

Keeping warm

Arctic wolves are bigger than other wolves. Their size helps them to keep warm in winter. Wolves in other habitats lose a lot of heat through their large ears and long noses. Arctic wolves have smaller ears and shorter snouts, to reduce heat loss. In summer, the wolf sheds its winter coat for a thinner, grey coat, which matches the rocks and soil.

 Arctic wolves can survive temperatures as cold as -40°C thanks to their dense fur.

Large prey

Hunting can be difficult in the icy landscape but the Arctic wolf can survive for weeks without food. Caribou and musk oxen are their favourite prey. A large pack is needed to bring down one of these powerful creatures.

Musk oxen calves make the easiest targets. But if the cattle catch the scent of a wolf pack, the adults form a circle with their babies in the middle. The musk oxen face outwards with horns lowered. Faced with a wall of horns, the wolves may be forced to retreat. They may have to settle for smaller prey such as ducks, hares or rodents.

VAST TERRITORIES

The size of a pack's territory is related to the amount of prey available. In the Arctic, prey is scarce. Animals such as the caribou wander long distances, while the wolves follow. So Arctic wolves hunt in a huge area – up to 13,000 square kilometres. That's an area nearly half the size of Belgium.

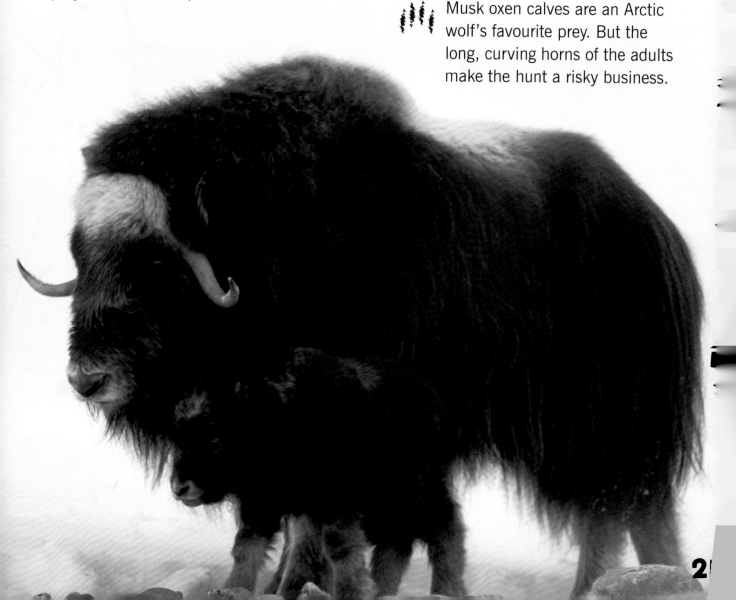

Musk oxen calves are an Arctic wolf's favourite prey. But the long, curving horns of the adults make the hunt a risky business.

Raising cubs

Only two animals breed in the wolf pack – the alpha male and female. If other wolves were to breed, the pack would get too big. Although the cubs are not their own, all pack members help to feed, guard and train them.

Mating and birth

Alpha wolves stay together for life. They breed in early spring. The pups are born two months later when the weather gets warmer. The she-wolf gives birth in a **den** – a cave or large burrow. Newborn wolves are tiny and quite helpless – they cannot see, hear or stand. They snuggle up to their mother and drink her milk.

Growing up

At one month old, the cubs wobble to the den entrance. They meet the rest of the pack and get their first glimpse of the outside world. They begin to eat half-chewed meat brought by the adult wolves. The cubs play in a safe place in the wolf territory. One adult guards them while the rest go hunting. At ten months old, the cubs join the hunt. At first, they just watch the adults to learn new skills.

These pups are drinking their mother's milk

Cubs have dark fuzzy fur

She-wolves usually give birth to five or six cubs, but there can be as many as a dozen.

Leaving home

Young wolves are fully grown by 18 months old. Young she-wolves reach breeding age at two years old, males at three years old. At this point, they become a threat to their parents and are often turned out of the pack. The young wolves wander alone or with their brothers or sisters until they meet other wolves and start a new pack.

PLAY-FIGHTING

Cubs spend a lot of time play-fighting. They rarely hurt one another, but fighting establishes a pecking order which mirrors the hierarchy in the wolf pack. As two cubs wrestle, the weaker rolls on its back to show it gives up. The winner stands tall with its tail high. One day it may lead its own pack.

Fighting builds strong muscles and teaches young wolves how to behave in a pack.

Wolves have a 'play-expression' to show the fight is not for real

Stronger cub

Weaker cub

Wolves and people

Wolves feature in stories and legends around the world. In fairy tales and horror films, they are shown as wicked creatures that prey on humans, especially children. But are wolves really as bad as they appear?

Big, bad wolf?

In real life, wolves are very wary of people and they rarely attack. Long ago, before guns were invented, they may have been bolder. Wolves tend to live far away from people, but they have been known to raid farms to steal chickens, sheep or calves. For this reason, farmers see wolves as enemies.

Wolves under threat

Over the centuries, wolves have been shot, poisoned, trapped and hunted with dogs. They have been killed for their fur, and sometimes for sport. Wolves are also put at risk when people take over the wild places where they live. In many areas, forests have been chopped down and wild grasslands fenced off to make fields and pastures. This means the wolves have less room to hunt and roam.

 This medieval illustration shows a wolf hunt. Noblemen on horses, helpers on foot and a pack of dogs are chasing a wolf.

Bring back the wolf

Wolves were once common throughout the north. Now they have been wiped out in many places, including Britain, most of western Europe and the USA. Recently however, wolves have started to make a comeback. People's attitudes to wolves have changed. Rather than being seen as pests, many people now admire wolves for qualities such as loyalty. Wolves bred in zoos have been released in some national parks in North America. For many people, wolves are a symbol of the wild. Like wild places, they are in need of our protection.

COYOTE COMEBACK

As wolves have been wiped out in the USA, coyotes have taken their place. About half the size of wolves, coyotes have very flexible feeding habits. They have now spread through much of North America, and even live close to towns. But they, too, steal chickens and sheep, and cause just as much trouble for farmers.

This Canadian wolf is being measured before it is released in Yellowstone National Park, USA, to bring wolves back to the area.

Rare wolves

Wolves were once the most widespread predator on land. Now some types of grey wolves, such as Mexican and Indian wolves, are in danger of dying out. Two close relatives of grey wolves, Simien wolves and red wolves, are also extremely rare.

Simien wolves

Simien wolves live in the highlands of Ethiopia in East Africa. This slim, coyote-sized wolf has a handsome reddish coat and long legs. Simien wolves mostly hunt alone, killing hares and rodents, but may band together to kill antelope. Unlike grey wolves, which mate within their pack, Simien wolves usually mate with animals from neighbouring packs.

Simien wolves are under threat because farmers have taken over the wild land where they live. People also shoot them for their fur or because they kill farm animals. Only a few hundred are left. Luckily, they mostly live in protected areas where hunting is forbidden.

There are only about 400 Simien wolves left in the wild. The fight is on to save this rare animal.

Simien wolves are also known as Ethiopian wolves

The red wolf

Another very rare wolf, the red wolf, comes from North America. It was once found throughout the southeastern USA. Settlers shot large numbers of red wolves because they threatened their farm animals. By the 1970s this wolf was **extinct** in the wild, but a handful were left in zoos. In the 1980s, wolf-lovers launched a campaign to save it. Red wolves were bred in zoos, and the young were released in two protected areas. There are now about 150 of these rare wolves.

MYSTERY IDENTITY?

Scientists disagree about the true nature of the red wolf. Some experts see it as a separate species, a cousin of the grey wolf. Others think it is a crossbreed between grey wolves and coyotes – in other words, a coy-wolf.

Red wolves live in protected areas in the wild.

Facts and records

Wolves may not be the world's fastest or largest predators, but they are among the most intelligent. Hunting in a pack, wolves are able to take on just about any creature they meet.

The Arctic wolf's thick fur and big body help it to keep warm in the cold winters.

Largest and smallest

- The biggest grey wolf is the Arctic wolf. It measures up to 2 metres long and can weigh 80 kg.

- The smallest grey wolves are steppe wolves and Arabian wolves. They measure about 80 cm long and can weigh as little as 12 kg.

Giant wolves

About two million years ago, huge wolves roamed North America. The dire wolf was half as big again as the average grey wolf. Packs of these fierce predators hunted prehistoric camels, rhinos and bison on grassy plains.

Body facts

- Wolf pups are born blind and deaf. Over half of wolf pups may not survive.

- A wolf's sense of smell is over 100 times greater than that of a human.

- Wolves can't sweat because they don't have sweat glands. If a wolf gets hot, it pants with its mouth open and its long, wet tongue hanging out. Moisture evaporates from the tongue and wet nose. This helps the wolf to keep cool.

These wolf pups will be very dependent on their mother for the first few months of life.

Did you know?

- Each wolf has an individual scent. As wolves roam in search of prey, they scent-mark their route with urine. By sniffing the trail of another wolf, a pack member can probably tell which animal it is following.

- With their large stomachs, wolves can eat up to 9 kg of meat at once. That's like eating a huge turkey on your own in one sitting!

Names and numbers

- The alpha male and female are the leaders of a wolf pack. 'Alpha' is the first letter of the Greek alphabet.

- Wolves are often on the move for 8–10 hours a day.

- Arctic wolves are able to survive up to five months darkness a year.

Glossary

alpha wolves
the name given to
the top male and
female in a wolf
pack, who lead
the others and are
usually the only
wolves that breed

beta wolves
wolves who are
second-in-command
in a wolf pack

body language
when an animal
holds its body in
a certain way, to
express its feelings
or status in a group

breed
to have young; also
a type of animal
such as a dog, which
has been developed
by breeding over
many years

caching
when an animal
hides food
for later

canid
a member of
the dog and
wolf family

carnivore
an animal that
eats meat

cub
a young wolf;
wolf cubs are
also called pups

den
the home of
an animal such
as a wolf

extinct
no longer
in existence,
having died out

facial
to do with the face

field of vision
the area an animal
can see without
turning its head

grazing
eating grass

guard hair
one of the long,
coarse hairs that
make up the outer
layer of a wolf's coat

habitat
a particular place
where plants and
animals live, such
as a forest or desert

hierarchy
a strict order within
a group in which
a leader makes
decisions for others

pack
a group of wolves
that live and
hunt together

predator
an animal that hunts
others for food

prey
an animal that is
eaten for food
by another

species
a particular type
of animal, such
as a grey wolf

streamlined
a smooth,
pointed shape

subspecies
a subgroup within
a species, such as
desert wolves

territory
an area where
an animal lives,
hunts and breeds,
and which it may
defend against
others of its kind

tundra
the treeless plains
of the far north

Index

Web finder

International Wolf Center
www.wolf.org/wolves/learn/justkids/kids.asp
Learn all about wolves and try out some fun wolf activities.

Wolfquest
www.wolfquest.org
Live the life of a wild wolf in the USA with this web-based video game.

Wolf Park Kids!
www.wolfparkkids.org/animals/wolfstuff.html
Find out more about wolves and try your hand at some wolf games.

Wolfweb
www.wolfweb.com/facts.html
Find out about wolves from the past, and how these creatures live today.

Defenders of Wildlife
www.defenders.org/programs_and_policy/wildlife_conservation/imperiled_species/wolves/wolf_facts
All you need to know about wolves and how you can help to save them.